SILVER
LINING
MOMENTS

A Practice of
Gratitude & Resilience

Kerry Raleigh

BALBOA.PRESS
A DIVISION OF HAY HOUSE

Balboa Press books may be ordered through booksellers or by contacting:

Balboa Press
A Division of Hay House
1663 Liberty Drive
Bloomington, IN 47403
www.balboapress.com
844-682-1282

Because of the dynamic nature of the Internet, any web addresses or links contained in this book may have changed since publication and may no longer be valid. The views expressed in this work are solely those of the author and do not necessarily reflect the views of the publisher, and the publisher hereby disclaims any responsibility for them.

The author of this book does not dispense medical advice or prescribe the use of any technique as a form of treatment for physical, emotional, or medical problems without the advice of a physician, either directly or indirectly. The intent of the author is only to offer information of a general nature to help you in your quest for emotional and spiritual well-being. In the event you use any of the information in this book for yourself, which is your constitutional right, the author and the publisher assume no responsibility for your actions.

Using such sites as QuoteInvestigator® at quoteinvestigator.com, Wikiquote at https://en.wikiquote.org/wiki/Main_Page; BrainyQuote at https://www.brainyquote.com, as well as reference articles and books of quotations, care has been taken to ensure the accuracy of the quotes used in this book. However, confirming the original source of a quote is not always simple or easy. In many instances, different resources have different conclusions. If you find any error, please feel free to email Kerry at Kerry@SilverLiningMoments.com.

Kerry Raleigh also hosts a podcast, Silver Lining Moments with Kerry. This podcast is found at http://silverliningmoments.libsyn.com and other podcast platforms. In addition to *Silver Lining Moments: A Practice of Gratitude & Resilience*, Kerry created The *BEING* Journal Series, including: *BEING in 2020, Releasing what it was like to BE in 2020 and Resetting into 2021 and beyond, Through Lists, Quotes, BE-oodles*™, *Quotes, Conversations and More!, BEING 13 in 13 Lists of 13, BEING 14 in 14 Lists of 14, BEING 15 in 15 Lists of 15, BEING 16 in 16 Lists of 16, BEING 17 in 17 Lists of 17,* and *BEING 18 in 18 Lists of 18*. The *BEING* Journals are available on Amazon.

Cover design by Shawn Bettencourt.

Print information available on the last page.

ISBN: 978-1-9822-6032-3 (sc)
ISBN: 978-1-9822-6033-0 (e)

Balboa Press rev. date: 05/06/2021

Silver Lining Moments: A Practice of Gratitude & Resilience

Blank writing pages for your Silver Lining Moments
Gratitude Feeling & Resilience Building Worksheets
And, some quotes for good thoughts and inspiration

* Spell check keeps telling me that this word is not spelled correctly. I think it is. Shouldn't there be a name for us who journal? We are the Journalers!

"If we had no winter,
the spring would not be so pleasant;
if we did not sometimes taste of adversity,
prosperity would not be so welcome."
- *Anne Bradstreet*

Acknowledgments & Appreciation

A Silver Lining Moment comes in many forms, including people. Many people are Silver Lining Moments in my life. To each and every one, thank you!

In choosing my 12 stories of Silver Lining Moments, I did not plan which stories to include. I had an intention to include Silver Lining Moments from the darkest of days and from the everyday. Then, I just wrote. These stories are a sampling of the Silver Lining Moments of my life. While some friends are mentioned in these stories, many are not. Those not mentioned in the stories in this Journal shine just as brightly in my life and my heart as those mentioned.

As I write this, I am filled with so much gratitude; my heart is swelling with love. I started to write the names of every person who has helped me, who has shown kindness to me, who has loved me, who has laughed with me, who has danced with me, who has walked with me (both figuratively and literally), who has dropped what they were doing to be with me when I was in a crumbled heap of tears, who showed up for me. It doesn't seem right to name just a few here and it would take so many pages to name them all. If you are reading this and you think this is referring to you, you are right. Thank you.

A big thank you goes to my niece, Cori Slaw. She helped me with the technical edit of this journal. She made something daunting doable. And, with her edits, she made this journal better!

I dedicate this *Silver Lining Moments* Journal to my Mom, JoAnn Dorsey. She has persevered through much hardship while extending much love to many. Her belief in me never wavered, even when I did not believe in myself. She is my first and my forever Silver Lining Moment.

Dear Fellow Journaler,

As you begin your *Silver Lining Moments Journal*, I want to thank you. Taking time for your inner healing and self-love adds light to the world. To fully appreciate this, I want to share two quotes with you. One is a Chinese proverb:

> If there is light in the soul,
> there will be beauty in the person.
> If there is beauty in the person,
> there will be harmony in the house.
> If there is harmony in the house,
> there will be order in the nation.
> If there is order in the nation,
> there will be peace in the world.

The other is from my friend Donna. As I began to share my personal losses and journey toward healing, I became self-conscious and questioned why, what, or how could I have anything to say that could help others – who did I think I was? Donna simply said "Your pain is my pain; my pain is your pain. Your healing is my healing; my healing is your healing. We are all connected."

When we add light—in ourselves, for ourselves—the light automatically shines in the world around us. By finding and celebrating your own Silver Lining Moments, you are adding love and light to your soul. And this, my dear friend, is one way you make a positive impact in our world. So, thank you for adding light to our world!

In this journal, there is brief description about Silver Lining Moments, some ways to use this journal, and stories of Silver Lining Moments from my life. The heart of Silver Lining Moments Journal is your writing and your Silver Lining Moment stories! It is my sincere wish that you find this journal entertaining, inspiring, and empowering as you find and celebrate your own Silver Lining Moments.

With kindness and gratitude,
Kerry

What is a Silver Lining Moment?

For every moment, there is a silver lining. May you see yours!

Just like every cloud,
every moment has a silver lining.

When we glance at a cloud with a silver lining, we mainly notice the cloud—the silver lining appears to be a small, thin lining around the cloud. But, when we look at it, *really* look at it, we see that the silver lining is the light that supports, surrounds, and fills up the entire space behind and around the cloud. The silver lining isn't a small lining; the silver lining has no bounds. The cloud is small. Clouds will come and go; the light is constant and is always there.

In life, we all have positive moments and negative moments; moments where love and laughter permeate our very being and moments where we are pulled down in despair, anger, frustration or sadness; moments where we feel connected and alive and moments where we feel alone and isolated. In these dark moments, the light is there even if we can barely see its flicker. When we focus on the light – the lessons learned, the friendships formed, the beliefs renewed, the love given, the nights held-on through, etc. – no matter how small it may appear, the flicker steadies and shines brighter. The unbearable moments become bearable. Just as with the cloud, the dark moments are blips that move away; and, when they do, we grow in the light.

For me, looking for and acknowledging the Silver Lining Moments has been a way of life – a part of who I am, or perhaps a habit I formed as a coping mechanism. I experienced many losses – the loss of my father after his death when I was 3 years old, the loss of innocence when I was molested at 11 years old, the loss of the belief that I was good enough for success when I was rejected from my dream college, the loss of 2 marriages from divorce, the loss of my savings, and, the hardest, the loss of all 5 of my babies through miscarriage. I know loss. I know despair. I know deep and utter sadness.

And, I know love and kindness, laughter and friendship, silliness and joy. In each of my darkest moments, there was someone showing me the light: friends who changed their weekend (Mother's Day) plans, made arrangements for their kids, flew from their state to mine so they could visit me at a time when I was feeling utterly un-loveable; a co-worker who bought me a Starbucks soy chai latte, my favorite drink, when I was feeling broke; a stranger who offered me a smile when I was on the brink of tears; a therapist who provided safety, support, and chocolate covered macadamia nuts; and many, many, more. The Silver Lining Moments far outnumber, outweigh, and out-value the cloudy and dark moments in my life.

In my personal life, I have gotten through some very hard times by looking for, and focusing on, the Silver Lining Moments. Sometimes, I felt like the Silver Lining Moment was a rope that I was hanging onto for dear life as it pulled me through a dark time. Other times, the Silver Lining Moment pushed me through as I dug in my heels, resisting growth or change. Each time, seeing the Silver Lining Moment helped me see the light in others and in myself. In seeing this light, I felt lighter.

Seeing the Silver Lining Moments does not mean ignoring the problems, darkness, and hardships, or pretending they did not happen. It is not about being naïve or looking through rose-colored glasses. It is looking at these moments, working through them, and knowing that you will be okay because you are more than the problem or darkness; <u>you are the light</u>.

A Silver Lining Moment takes many forms:

- A lesson learned
- A serendipitous coincidence
- An act of kindness
- An unexpected good out of a bad situation
- A good laugh
- A joke from the difficulty of an absurd situation
- A sense of empathy and compassion
- A renewed belief in humanity
- A community coming together to help one another
- A lifelong bond formed from having gone through something together
- A positive change in someone's behavior or attitude...maybe even your own

There is simply no limit on how Silver Lining Moments show up. But, they always do because Silver Lining Moments, like the light behind a cloud, are always there.

No matter the form, recognizing and celebrating the Silver Lining Moments develop gratitude and build resilience:

GRATITUDE
for feeling the warmth of the light (in whatever form)
shining on you just when you needed it;

RESILIENCE
from the knowledge that you can get through the
dark moments because you already have.

In your gratitude and resilience, you are intensifying the light in your soul and expanding it outward to your house, nation, and world.

"If you are seeking, seek us with joy
For we live in the kingdom of joy.
Do not give your heart to anything else
But to the love of those who are clear joy,
Do not stray into the neighborhood of despair.
For there are hopes: they are real, they exist –
Do not go in the direction of darkness –
I tell you: suns exist."
- *Rumi*

Using This Journal

This is *your* Silver Lining Moments Journal. There is no right or wrong way to use it. However you use this Journal is the perfect way for you.

In this Journal, I share 12 of my Silver Lining Moment stories. At the bottom of each story, I write the place and date as to when the story took place. These stories may trigger a memory or feeling for you. If so, write about it. The blank pages between each Silver Lining Moment story are for you to write about a Silver Lining Moment from your own life. You will find a simple statement – "A moment of _____ is lined by _____" – on top of each page for you to complete, should you wish. Or, use these pages to write about whatever comes to your mind.

After each Silver Lining Moment story, there are Gratitude Feeling & Resilience Building worksheets. Take a moment to acknowledge and celebrate seeing your Silver Lining Moments. Write what you're thankful for and how you were resilient. In your gratitude and resilience, you are expanding your light. Better pick up a pair of sunglasses along the way, my friend, because you shine — your light is strong and bright!

Here are some ways to start a *Silver Lining Moments* Practice:

❖ How many Silver Lining Moments do you have? Sit down for a set amount of time, say one hour, and see how many Silver Lining Moments you can come up with from your own life. In this first hour, just write the basics for each moment. Then throughout the month, you can delve into these moments further. I bet you will be amazed at how many Silver Lining Moments you come up with during this hour!

❖ What's Your Silver Lining Moment today? For 30 days, write about a Silver Lining Moment from each day. If you enjoyed this practice, repeat for another 30 days or make it a daily practice.

- ❖ How many silver linings do you have for one moment? Take one incident, one cloudy moment in your life, and see how many silver linings you have just for that moment. If it is a particularly dark moment, write about it for several days. Look at it from all angles and feelings. How many lessons did you learn? How did you grow? Who showed up to support you? Who left you?

- ❖ Set a monthly date with yourself. Write in this Journal once a month for one whole year. Reflect on and celebrate your Silver Lining Moments at the end of each month as you start the next one.

- ❖ Just write. Whatever comes to your mind, write it in your Journal. If you are stuck or do not know where to start, you can always simply write:

   "There is a silver lining to this moment of _____, and I will see it when I am ready", or

   "I am grateful for the silver lining to this moment of _____ ".

- ❖ Connect. Look for Silver Lining Moments with Kerry on social media and at www.SilverLiningMoments.com

If there is a dark moment in your life and you cannot see the silver lining, that is okay. If the thought of that moment brings you sadness, fear, or anger, write about those feelings. I encourage you to write about it deeply, fully, and honestly. If you find that you are stuck in a specific feeling or story, I strongly encourage you to get help, see a professional therapist, meet with a personal coach, or attend a personal development/ healing workshop. Sometimes, we all need help to heal our pain and move forward. I know I sure did! When you heal yourself, you shine inward and outward – you add light to the world.

Remember, finding the silver lining does not mean that the dark moment, the trauma, or the wrong that someone did to you was okay. It means that **you are okay** even though this happened. It means that you have grown, you have learned something, you are stronger than the dark moment, you are connected to the light. You are resilient!

"All our talents increase in the using, and every faculty,
both good and bad, *strengthens* by *exercise*."
- Ann Brontë
(Emphasis added.)

For me, finding the Silver Lining Moments is a practice – an exercise that strengthens gratitude and resilience. Finding silver linings in the day to day matters strengthens our gratitude and resilience "muscles". The more we exercise these "muscles", the stronger they become. With regular practice, our gratitude and resilience will be strong and will hold us together – even as we pass through dark moments. To reflect this, this *Silver Lining Moments: A Practice of Gratitude & Resilience* Journal is filled with Silver Lining Moments surrounding some of my day to day matters as well as those surrounding my darkest moments.

This Journal is not about my *Silver Lining Moments* practice; it's about yours. My Silver Lining Moment stories and the *Gratitude Feeling & Resilience Building* worksheets are here to keep you company during your practice. Think of them as your exercise and training partner – a reminder that you are not alone. So, batter-up; hut, hut, hike; tee-it up; pick up the baton; come to the center of your yoga mat; [insert here any other sport or exercise reference for "get ready"]; and start your own *Silver Lining Moments* practice. Grab a pen, write your *Silver Lining Moments* – exercise your gratitude and resilience muscles – and watch your light beam stronger and farther, inward and outward. Feel that? It's your own brilliant glow!

"My barn having burned down,
I can now see the moon."
- *Mizuta Masahide*

A moment of DISRUPTION is lined by COMPLETION

_____

"Other than that Mrs. Lincoln, how was the play?" This question, slightly changed, could be asked to each of us about 2020. Other than THAT [Covid-19; daily virus infection and death counts; care home, hospital, and healthcare overload; closed schools, restaurants, and businesses; natural disasters; fires; hurricanes; earthquakes; police shootings; protests, counter-protests, riots, looting; conspiracy theories; killer hornet invasions (what???)...], how was your 2020?

This morning, I read that 1,000 people died of Covid in the US yesterday, and over 1,000,000 people were tested positive for Covid in the US last week. I felt dazed. This is just one day and one week in one country. I thought of the total numbers (easier to think of numbers instead of people) who had Covid, who died from it, who knew someone who died from it. Dazed, I feel like falling into a void. While no one in my immediate family has had Covid, it is creeping closer to this inner circle as I learn about family members of friends having Covid, some dying from it. Fear fills the void.

I snap out of it as my day begins. I do a yoga video. I think about this Silver Lining Moment story, which I started last week. Was this story making light of people's hardships, fears, and losses of 2020? How can I honor the gravity of 2020 with my Silver Lining Moment practice? And, just now, in a brief pause of typing, I say to myself- this is what it is all about. Acknowledging the dark times and finding the good in them to pull you through into the light. This is why it is a practice.

So, acknowledging the clouds in my 2020, I acknowledge the unsettled anxiety I felt as my world and the whole world was disrupted, and the fear I had from not having health insurance. My husband and I were scheduled to return to China in March 2020 to teach. This would have allowed us to save money toward our dream of buying our own home in Spain in a few years. After living as digital nomads since April of 2018,

1

we were ready to settle down and build our future. After starting what I call my PAUSE & RESET Journey in 2016, I finally had clarity of purpose and vision for the projects that I wanted do. Teaching in China would help me save money while also giving me time to work on these projects. I was ready to press PLAY on my RESET.

But 2020 was forcing the whole world to pause – forcing us to reset the way we live and think. For my husband and me, we had to pause our plans with uncertainty as to where and how we would live. He is a UK citizen and I am US citizen; we had been traveling throughout 2018 and 2019; we didn't have our own apartment or home; and there were time limits on how long we could stay in each other's home country and travel restrictions on where we could go. We were unsettled in every sense of the word.

After a stay in Greece, I returned to the US to get my work visa for China and my husband returned to the UK to get his. I got my visa before he did so our plan was for me to meet him in the UK and then we would fly to China together. I arrived in the UK on March 10. The next day, the UK issued travel restrictions against US citizens. As the week unfolded and as more world travel restrictions went up, it became clear that we were not heading to China anytime soon.

Instead of teaching in China and saving money toward our dream, we found ourselves living with my in-laws in England for seven months. They live in a nice terrace home that is spacious for two people but a little tight for four. For some perspective on this, one night, my stomach got violently upset at a time when one of my in-laws was in the only bathroom. I had no choice but to run to the back garden and throw-up repeatedly with projectile vomit. Loud heaving and vomiting retching sounds filled the air as I crumbled over and cried. (Yes, I can be bit a melodramatic but who doesn't cry when they throw-up?) I wonder what the neighbors were thinking!?

Now, there was also Sunday dinners, shopping and coffee/tea with my mother-in-law, and my father-in-law's stories. Their home is filled with a stable and calming energy. While we all did our best to give each other space, our feet may have all been a slightly bruised as we were stepping on each other's toes. I know years from now I will look back at this time with my husband and his parents fondly. Heck, it's just been a month since we were there and I already feel the fondness and gratitude for my in-laws and our time there.

My visa, including its month-long Covid extension, expired. We needed to leave the UK. I missed my parents and my family but going to the US was not a viable option. Namely, I didn't want to get exposed to Covid while traveling and then expose it to my family. Instead, my husband and I traveled to Albania where we could afford to rent our own apartment and self-isolate. It was an unexpected turn to our 2020 but we are safe and we have our own place overlooking the Adriatic Sea. As our pause continues, we are in a pretty good place to press the PLAY button.

It is in our AirBNB apartment where my Silver Lining Moment for 2020 came to me. In this apartment, I completed a 30-day yoga series. It took me 60 days to complete, but I completed it! This may not sound like a huge thing but for me it was monumental! This was the first time that I completed a series of this type, despite starting many, over many years. Here are just a few:

- 21-Day Meditation Series with Deepak Chopra and Oprah (about five of these): they were so calming and grounding that I never made it past the 11th day;
- 7-Week Daily Om Course, Intimacy without Responsibility: I learned so much that truly changed the way I am in relationships for the better that I stopped after the second week;
- 30 Days of Good Karma: This came in a small cardboard box with holes to punch in like an advent calendar with each hole containing a good karma-building activity. A friend got me this

when I was going through my second divorce. I loved this gift; it gave me something to look forward to each day, at a time when I struggled to just get through the day. I made it to day 17;

- 30-Day Love Your Life with Mike Dooley of TUT (The Universe Talks): I loved this so much that I stopped at around the 10th day when I got to liking my life;
- 30-Day Manifesting Challenge: I completed about only 21 days but boy was I on track to manifesting my manifesting;
- And, many, many, many…..many, many, many MORE!

Each one of my #-Day Challenges or Activities was aimed at empowering one with self-love and all that. I never finished them just like I never saw many of my ideas to completion. While I got plenty of good from the parts that I did complete, there was a sneaky little undercurrent of failure at not completing things. This undercurrent of failure met with not-good-enough and the two of them subtly ran through my veins and seemed to clog any path to my success and prosperity – of seeing my ideas realized and projects completed.

When I finished the 30 Days of Yoga and closed the YouTube video, it was as if I was standing in front of the Failure and Not-Good-Enough buddies in my veins; holding a stop sign, and declaring, "Well, NOT anymore! It's time for you both to be on your way….with love and kindness be transformed!" I was beaming as I told my husband that I completed this video series. Later that week, I completed the guided journal, *BEING in 2020, Releasing what it was like to BE in 2020, Resetting into 2021 and beyond, Through Lists, Be-oodles™, Quotes, Conversations and More!* And, with this story, I am completing this journal, *Silver Lining Moments: A Practice of Gratitude & Resilience.* You reading this is evidence of completion! I began the *Silver Lining Moments* journal in December of 2017 and *The BEING Journals* series in September of 2018. It was in 2020 that I completed them both. What's Next?

As I look at 2020, I see two major themes for me: disruption and completion. As the saying goes, life happens while you are busy making other plans.* In this year of 2020, my ability to make any plans was disrupted. In this disruption, life happened and I completed things.

**From 2020, I discovered how a moment of
disruption is lined by completion.**

England & Albania @ 2020

---

* This saying has been expressed in different ways by different people over the centuries including Allen Saunders and John Lennon. See https://quoteinvestigator. com/2012/05/06/other-plans/

Gratitude Feeling & Resilience Building

From this moment of disruption lined by completion:

GRATITUDE

I am grateful for: **my parents' well-being; my in-laws; the UK customs agent who granted my entrance just a day before the border closings; Facetime with my Mom and my sisters; my sister Kelly helping my parents so much during the quarantine and throughout 2020; my husband's quick wit and sense of humor; Sunday dinners; family and friends; SLM podcast guests; good health and time.**

RESILIENCE

My ability to recover from a difficulty, to overcome a challenge, to get up after a fall – my resilience – is evident in: **my eating white-button mushrooms (even though I can't stand mushrooms), drinking green tea, and picking-up other habits that support good health; my using meditation, journaling, and yoga to ground me when triggered by conspiracy theories, fake news, and other current events; in going with the flow from the US to UK to Albania, and in COMPLETING yoga, Being Journals, and this SLM Journal :)**

With gratitude and resilience, **I feel calm and safe; I can exhale.**

> *"The human mind always makes progress, but it is a progress in spirals."*
> – Germaine Necker, Madame de Staël

Silver Lining Moments
By Kerry Raleigh

From raindrops to rainbows
A Silver Lining grows
Sometimes it is hard to see
And we may fall to our knees
Sometimes it shines so bright
That our hearts are filled with light
As clouds drift in and as they move away
Over time we know that every MOMENT
of every day
Has within it a SILVER LINING
that stays

What's your Silver Lining Moment?

A moment of _____ **is lined by** _____ .

_____

_____

_____

_____

_____

_____

_____

_____

_____

_____

_____

_____

_____

_____

_____

_____

_____

_____

_____

_____

_____

_____

_____

_____

_____

A moment of _____ **is lined by** _____.

_____

_____

_____

_____

_____

_____

_____

_____

_____

_____

_____

_____

_____

_____

_____

_____

_____

_____

_____

_____

_____

_____

_____

_____

_____

_____

A moment of _____ **is lined by** _____.

_____

_____

_____

_____

_____

_____

_____

_____

_____

_____

_____

_____

_____

_____

_____

_____

_____

_____

_____

_____

_____

_____

_____

A moment of _____ **is lined by** _____.

_____

_____

_____

_____

_____

_____

_____

_____

_____

_____

_____

_____

_____

_____

_____

_____

_____

_____

_____

_____

_____

_____

_____

_____

A moment of _____ **is lined by** _____.

_____

_____

_____

_____

_____

_____

_____

_____

_____

_____

_____

_____

_____

_____

_____

_____

_____

_____

_____

_____

_____

_____

_____

_____

_____

A moment of _____ is lined by _____.

_____

_____

_____

_____

_____

_____

_____

_____

_____

_____

_____

_____

_____

_____

_____

_____

_____

_____

_____

_____

_____

_____

_____

_____

A moment of _____ **is lined by** _____.

_____

_____

_____

_____

_____

_____

_____

_____

_____

_____

_____

_____

_____

_____

_____

_____

_____

_____

_____

_____

_____

_____

_____

_____

A moment of _____ **is lined by** _____.

_____

_____

_____

_____

_____

_____

_____

_____

_____

_____

_____

_____

_____

_____

_____

_____

_____

_____

_____

_____

_____

_____

_____

A moment of _____ **is lined by** _____.

_____

_____

_____

_____

_____

_____

_____

_____

_____

_____

_____

_____

_____

_____

_____

_____

_____

_____

_____

_____

_____

_____

_____

_____

Gratitude Feeling & Resilience Building

_____

From this moment of _____
lined by _____:

GRATITUDE

I am grateful for: _____

_____

_____

_____

RESILIENCE

My ability to recover from a difficulty, to overcome a challenge, to get
up after a fall – my resilience – is evident in: _____

_____

_____

_____

With gratitude and resilience, _____

_____

_____

_____

"Fire is the test of gold;
adversity, of strong men."
- *Seneca ('the Younger')*

A moment of CONGESTED AND FACELESS TRAFFIC is lined by HUMANITY AND KINDNESS

I was driving in rush hour traffic on the always-chaotic Route 95 from Miami to Hollywood Beach, Florida. The rain was pouring down – one of those torrential tropical rains that native-Floridians know all too well. As a newcomer to Florida, this torrential rain, on this chaotic, congested road was downright terrifying. Then, my car started to slow down even though I was pressing on the gas. I managed to pull alongside the center meridian as my car just stopped.

Within seconds, before any panic or fear could set in, I saw a tow-truck pull over in front of me and back up to my car. The driver hooked up my car and motioned for me to get in his truck. As I was walking to his truck, I was amazed at the speed of the Florida State Highway system. This must be one of the advantages of living in a big city – immediate roadside assistance.

After I was in his truck for bit and as we were talking, I was telling him how impressed I was with Florida's roadside assistance. He gave me a quizzical look. It slowly dawned on me that he was not part of an official roadside assistance program. He was just some guy who had a job delivering cars from north Florida to south Florida. He had just dropped cars off in Miami and was heading back north when he saw my car on the side of the road. He did not hesitate at all; he quickly stopped to help me.

For a split second, I realized I was in a car with a stranger and a brief flash of all the horror stories of men taking women captive in cars flashed across my mind. I took a breath and checked-in with this situation. I had nothing to fear.

During a torrential Florida rain, in the middle of congested and agitated Miami traffic, a stranger stopped to help someone. He did not accept any money. He simply smiled as he dropped my car and me off safely at my apartment building. As he did, my confidence in guardian angels, kindness and humanity strengthened.

On I-95, I discovered how a moment of congested and faceless traffic is lined by humanity and kindness.

Miami, Florida @ 1999

Gratitude Feeling & Resilience Building

From this moment of congested and faceless traffic lined by humanity and kindness:

GRATITUDE

I am grateful for: **the kindness of strangers; getting to the side of the road and off the highway safe and sound as my car broke down; getting my car towed to my apartment.**

RESILIENCE

My ability to recover from a difficulty, to overcome a challenge, to get up after a fall – my resilience – is evident in: **not panicking; calming my nerves when I felt anxious; getting my car safely to the side of the road in traffic and in the rain.**

With gratitude and resilience, **I feel happy and strong. I can trust in the good in others.**

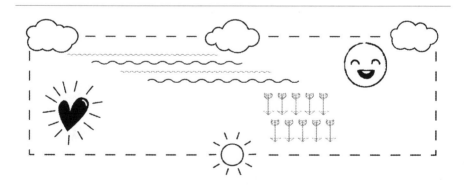

Silver Lining Moments

By Kerry Raleigh

From raindrops to rainbows
A Silver Lining grows
Sometimes it is hard to see
And we may fall to our knees
Sometimes it shines so bright
That our hearts are filled with light
As clouds drift in and as they move away
Over time we know that every MOMENT
of every day
Has within it a SILVER LINING
that stays

What's your Silver Lining Moment?

A moment of _____ **is lined by** _____.

_____

_____

_____

_____

_____

_____

_____

_____

_____

_____

_____

_____

_____

_____

_____

_____

_____

_____

_____

_____

_____

_____

_____

_____

_____

A moment of _____ is lined by _____.

_____

_____

_____

_____

_____

_____

_____

_____

_____

_____

_____

_____

_____

_____

_____

_____

_____

_____

_____

_____

_____

_____

_____

A moment of _____ **is lined by** _____ .

_____

_____

_____

_____

_____

_____

_____

_____

_____

_____

_____

_____

_____

_____

_____

_____

_____

_____

_____

_____

_____

_____

_____

_____

A moment of _____ is lined by _____.

_____

_____

_____

_____

_____

_____

_____

_____

_____

_____

_____

_____

_____

_____

_____

_____

_____

_____

_____

_____

_____

_____

A moment of _____ **is lined by** _____.

_____

_____

_____

_____

_____

_____

_____

_____

_____

_____

_____

_____

_____

_____

_____

_____

_____

_____

_____

_____

_____

_____

A moment of _____ is lined by _____.

_____

_____

_____

_____

_____

_____

_____

_____

_____

_____

_____

_____

_____

_____

_____

_____

_____

_____

_____

_____

_____

_____

_____

_____

A moment of _____ **is lined by** _____.

_____

_____

_____

_____

_____

_____

_____

_____

_____

_____

_____

_____

_____

_____

_____

_____

_____

_____

_____

_____

_____

_____

_____

_____

A moment of _____ is lined by _____.

A moment of _____ **is lined by** _____.

_____

_____

_____

_____

_____

_____

_____

_____

_____

_____

_____

_____

_____

_____

_____

_____

_____

_____

_____

_____

_____

_____

_____

_____

_____

Gratitude Feeling & Resilience Building

_____

From this moment of _____

lined by _____:

GRATITUDE

I am grateful for: _____

_____

_____

_____

RESILIENCE

My ability to recover from a difficulty, to overcome a challenge, to get up after a fall – my resilience – is evident in: _____

_____

_____

_____

With gratitude and resilience, _____

_____

_____

_____

"I have not failed. I've just found 10,000 ways that won't work."
- Thomas A. Edison

"Ever tried. Ever failed. No matter.
Try again. Fail again. Fail better."
- *Samuel Beckett*

A moment of EPIC CAREER FAILURE
is lined by RESPECT

This is a recurring scene that I have lived out since July 2011. I am in the shower washing my hair. In my mind, I am arguing an evidentiary hearing before the court. I come up with different winning arguments. I go through my closing argument…again. I turn off the water, shake the water off my arms and legs, and shake my head in frustrated disgust – the trial ended 7 years ago! I didn't get the evidence in then--why am I still thinking about it?!

I bet most lawyers have one or two cases that just stay with them. This is one of mine. I had worked on this case for over four years. The clients, an elderly couple, became quite dear to me. During these four years, I was with them as he had to get his monthly eye injections for his macular degeneration, and as she had to go check to see if her cancer was still in remission. No matter the time or day, I always took their calls. I literally worked on their case day and night.

By the time this case went to trial, it had gained the attention of some media. A producer for a courtroom TV program sought and got permission to video record the trial. This case wasn't just being judged by the jury; I was being judged as a lawyer.

On the last day of trial, the jury deliberated for over 5 hours. I remember walking along the corridor with my boss while the jury was still deliberating. He asked "Do you think the jury's long deliberation is a bad sign?" Moments later the jury came back with a verdict of about $1.5 million dollars, which, unfortunately, was a far cry from the $4,000,000 that would have made my clients whole. I looked at my clients when the verdict came in. Their eyes just filled up with tears. They had spent 4 of their remaining twilight years fighting for justice and they felt like they got hit by the justice system. I felt like I got hit in the gut. I had let them down.

Everyone saw this as a failure – my boss, my clients, and most of all me. The next day, I walked into the office barely able to hold my head up. As I walked past the office of a colleague, an attorney who I respected a lot, she called me into her office. She sincerely congratulated me. She knew I felt disappointed but she reminded me how hard I had worked on the case and how difficult the issues in the case were. She acknowledged that a million dollar plus verdict was a big deal. She said she was proud of me. She was not sugar coating it. She was speaking frankly and hoped I could see it the same way. With each of her words, the heaviness of failure that I placed on my shoulders was lifted. I had earned the respect of someone who I respected. I walked out of her office with my head held high.

And on this morning, as I shake my head in frustrated disgust, I hear her words again and the self-disgust and frustration shake off again. You know what? I did okay then. It is okay that I think about it now. And, it is okay to let that sense of failure go and stand in self-respect.

In the words of a co-worker, I discovered how a moment of epic career failure is lined by respect.

Palm Beach, Florida 2011

Gratitude Feeling & Resilience Building

From this moment of epic career failure lined by respect:

GRATITUDE

I am grateful for: **all the lessons this case taught me about lawyering and about myself; for getting knocked off course so I could see that it wasn't the right course for me; for Janet's words and belief in me at a time I didn't believe in myself; these words pulled me through then and several times since.**

RESILIENCE

My ability to recover from a difficulty, to overcome a challenge, to get up after a fall – my resilience – is evident in: **my work ethic and dedication to those clients and to my clients after that case; starting my own firm, and then starting a new path in life.**

With gratitude and resilience, **I feel proud and okay to try new things**

Silver Lining Moments
By Kerry Raleigh

From raindrops to rainbows
A Silver Lining grows
Sometimes it is hard to see
And we may fall to our knees
Sometimes it shines so bright
That our hearts are filled with light
As clouds drift in and as they move away
Over time we know that every MOMENT
of every day
Has within it a SILVER LINING
that stays

What's your Silver Lining Moment?

A moment of _____ **is lined by** _____.

_____

_____

_____

_____

_____

_____

_____

_____

_____

_____

_____

_____

_____

_____

_____

_____

_____

_____

_____

_____

_____

_____

_____

A moment of _____ **is lined by** _____.

_____

_____

_____

_____

_____

_____

_____

_____

_____

_____

_____

_____

_____

_____

_____

_____

_____

_____

_____

_____

_____

_____

_____

A moment of _____ **is lined by** _____.

A moment of _____ **is lined by** _____.

A moment of _____ is lined by _____.

A moment of _____ **is lined by** _____.

_____

_____

_____

_____

_____

_____

_____

_____

_____

_____

_____

_____

_____

_____

_____

_____

_____

_____

_____

_____

_____

_____

_____

_____

_____

A moment of _____ **is lined by** _____.

_____

_____

_____

_____

_____

_____

_____

_____

_____

_____

_____

_____

_____

_____

_____

_____

_____

_____

_____

_____

_____

_____

A moment of _____ is lined by _____.

_____

_____

_____

_____

_____

_____

_____

_____

_____

_____

_____

_____

_____

_____

_____

_____

_____

_____

_____

_____

_____

_____

A moment of _____ **is lined by** _____.

Gratitude Feeling & Resilience Building

_____

From this moment of _____
lined by _____:

GRATITUDE

I am grateful for: _____

_____

_____

_____

RESILIENCE

My ability to recover from a difficulty, to overcome a challenge, to get up after a fall – my resilience – is evident in: _____

_____

_____

_____

With gratitude and resilience, _____

_____

_____

_____

"All God's angels come to us disguised."
- James Russell Lowell

A moment of DESPAIR is lined by ANGELS

My day started with my then husband telling me that he made up his mind and wanted a divorce. We were at a weekend couple's retreat-workshop. He refused to attend the rest of the workshop. It was a Saturday, the day before my 33rd birthday. I was pregnant for the 4th time. My first three pregnancies ended in miscarriage.

I remember lying in bed all day, just staring out the window, in a hopeless state. If I miscarried, I would lose another baby and the loss of another baby seemed too much to bear. If I did not miscarry, I would be bringing a baby into a broken home, something that I never wanted. There was no happy ending. So, I just laid in bed, staring out the hotel window, not wanting to move.

A few weeks later, just a few days before Thanksgiving, I lost my fourth baby.

I felt like the shell of a person with no core left and the shell felt like it was about to crack and crumble any minute.

A few weeks later, I was once again lying in my bed with no will to get out of it. It was a Friday and I should have already been at work. Yet, I remained in bed thinking – "well, I can't kill myself because that would hurt my Mom. But, if someone wanted to come in my home and kill me that would be okay." Despair defies logic. Before that thought could take hold, my phone rang. It was my executive assistant adamantly telling me that I needed to get to the office for a meeting right now. She stayed on the phone with me until I got out of bed.

Within minutes of getting in my car, my dear friend, Deanna, called. Although we were close friends, we did not talk that much. She said that she called because she wanted to let me know that I would be okay, that I was loved, and that she was thinking of me. After Deanna, my sister Kathy called me, then my Mom. Once I got to work, there was a meeting, bosses, deadlines. After work, I was heading to a personal development weekend retreat. There were no quiet times for deadly thoughts to lurk and linger.

At the personal development workshop, I was introduced to a roomful of people referred to as "angels" who had previously completed the workshop and came to support the other participants and me. Walking into the room, I was hesitant, sad, and a lost soul. Right as I entered the room, an Angel greeted me with a big smile and instant friendship. (We are still friends over 15 years later!) As the Angels filled the room with laughter, tears, and support, they filled me up with unconditional love. With their unconditional love, they held space for all the participants. In this space, I found a glimmer of myself and felt a hint of joy.

The Angels at the workshop were not the only angels that day. Each person who called me that day kept the lurking dark thoughts at bay -- each one was a light in the darkness guiding me along. As I filled up with the support of these angels, the despair left and the healing process began. And, I eventually came to see my miscarried babies as guardian angels who came to me to help me recalibrate the course of my life's journey.

In my greatest losses, I discovered how a moment of despair is lined by angels.

Vermont and South Florida @ 2005

Gratitude Feeling & Resilience Building

From this moment of falling into despair lined by angels:

GRATITUDE

I am grateful for: **being loved and all who love me; for the work meeting; for the calls from Ellen, Deanna, Kathy, and my Mom; for the TLC personal development weekend, Alice, Leif and all the angels; for God watching over me that day.**

RESILIENCE

My ability to recover from a difficulty, to overcome a challenge, to get up after a fall – my resilience – is evident in: **my not sinking into despair, attending the retreat and in trusting in the process, in smiling, playing, and dancing again**

With gratitude and resilience, **I feel alive!**

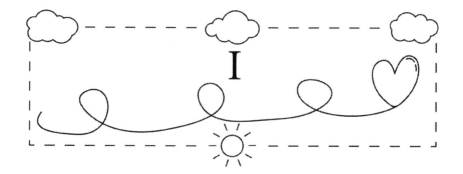

Silver Lining Moments

By Kerry Raleigh

From raindrops to rainbows
A Silver Lining grows
Sometimes it is hard to see
And we may fall to our knees
Sometimes it shines so bright
That our hearts are filled with light
As clouds drift in and as they move away
Over time we know that every MOMENT
of every day
Has within it a SILVER LINING
that stays

What's your Silver Lining Moment?

A moment of _____ **is lined by** _____.

_____

_____

_____

_____

_____

_____

_____

_____

_____

_____

_____

_____

_____

_____

_____

_____

_____

_____

_____

_____

_____

_____

A moment of _____ **is lined by** _____.

_____

_____

_____

_____

_____

_____

_____

_____

_____

_____

_____

_____

_____

_____

_____

_____

_____

_____

_____

_____

_____

_____

_____

_____

_____

A moment of _____ **is lined by** _____.

_____

_____

_____

_____

_____

_____

_____

_____

_____

_____

_____

_____

_____

_____

_____

_____

_____

_____

_____

_____

_____

_____

_____

A moment of _____ is lined by _____.

_____

_____

_____

_____

_____

_____

_____

_____

_____

_____

_____

_____

_____

_____

_____

_____

_____

_____

_____

_____

_____

_____

_____

A moment of _____ is lined by _____.

_____

_____

_____

_____

_____

_____

_____

_____

_____

_____

_____

_____

_____

_____

_____

_____

_____

_____

_____

_____

_____

_____

_____

_____

_____

A moment of _____ **is lined by** _____.

_____

_____

_____

_____

_____

_____

_____

_____

_____

_____

_____

_____

_____

_____

_____

_____

_____

_____

_____

_____

_____

_____

_____

_____

A moment of _____ **is lined by** _____ .

_____

_____

_____

_____

_____

_____

_____

_____

_____

_____

_____

_____

_____

_____

_____

_____

_____

_____

_____

_____

_____

_____

_____

A moment of _____ **is lined by** _____.

A moment of _____ **is lined by** _____.

_____

_____

_____

_____

_____

_____

_____

_____

_____

_____

_____

_____

_____

_____

_____

_____

_____

_____

_____

_____

_____

_____

Gratitude Feeling & Resilience Building

_____

From this moment of _____
lined by _____:

GRATITUDE

I am grateful for: _____

_____

_____

_____

RESILIENCE

My ability to recover from a difficulty, to overcome a challenge, to get
up after a fall – my resilience – is evident in: _____

_____

_____

_____

With gratitude and resilience, _____

_____

_____

_____

"Keep your face always toward
the sunshine
and the shadows will fall behind you."
- a Maori Proverb*

* A similar phrase was also in a poem "Youth and Age" published in 1850 by Charles Swain, and credit for this phrase has also been given to M.B. Whitman, Walt Whitman, and later to Helen Keller 1927.
See:www.quoteinvestigator.com

A moment of SELF-DEFEAT is lined by DISCOVERY

Cobblestone streets, whizzing motorcycles, and trattoria-lined streets filled one big maze as I was rushing to meet my study abroad group at the bus station in Florence, Italy. When I finally found the bus station, I could not find the bus. I was walking up and down rows of buses, looking up and down, but no one looked familiar. I was lost. In a foreign city. Again.

This was the second stage of my study abroad in the summer of 1997, and my first time traveling abroad by myself. The first stage was in Paris where I visited some longtime family friends who I had not seen since I was a young child. Paris may be the City of Lights, but for me, it was a maze. From the moment that I landed in Paris, I was lost. First, I got lost in the airport as I tried to figure my way out of he airport to the city center. Second, after searching for the Louvre, for what felt like hours (but was probably less than half of one), and with jet lag taking hold, I gave up and took a nap on a bench in some park. To my surprise, when I woke up an hour or so later, I realized that I was just facing the wrong direction. The Louvre was right behind me on the other side of a small grassy knoll; all I had to do was turn around and stand tall. Third, on my way to Versailles, I was seconds from getting on the wrong train. Save the grace of a little elderly lady who took me under her wing and guided me to the right train, who knows where I would have ended up. All my getting lost aside, I loved my stay in Paris and all the Parisians who greeted me with kindness as I aimlessly wondered its streets.

Now, in the second stage of my study abroad experience, I was in Florence, Italy where I was taking my courses. On this particular day, my school had organized a tour of Cinque Terre and the beautiful seaside mountain areas. I never found the bus. Later, a classmate said that he saw me as the bus was pulling away but the bus driver would not stop. Feeling bad, he got me a postcard from the area. The place looked beautiful!

In the first moments of missing the bus, I felt defeated and berated myself for my lack of direction. Most of all, I felt alone. I went back to my apartment, flopped on the couch, and just closed my eyes. With a few minutes of rest and some tears, I slowly opened my eyes, looked outside, and saw a beautiful bright summer day. Without any direction or plan, I began what I do so well – aimlessly wander. And, I had one of the best days of my life!

On that day, I discovered some of my favorite spots in Florence where I would return many times during my program. I waved to locals, chatted with people in that broken English and gesturing used by native English speakers and international travelers the world over, and exchanged many smiles with many Florentine locals. As I wandered from one side of Florence to another, I was filled with pure joy and unconditional love. As corny as it may sound, it was one of those moments that I felt connected in unconditional love with every other being – if I had put my hand out, I am sure a small bird would have landed on it! This day, this moment, has stayed with me over 20 years later. It is one of my happy places!!!

From getting lost (repeatedly), I discovered how a moment of self-defeat is lined by discovery.

Florence, Italy @ 1997

Gratitude Feeling & Resilience Building

From this moment of self-defeat lined by discovery:

GRATITUDE

I am grateful for: **the postcard from my classmate, for the sunshine that beckoned me outside, for Piazzale Michelangelo & San Miniato al Monte**

RESILIENCE

My ability to recover from a difficulty, to overcome a challenge, to get up after a fall – my resilience – is evident in: **getting off the couch, walking outside, and soaking up the sun's warmth.**

With gratitude and resilience, **I feel like an adventurer, anything is possible!**

"The best way out is always through."

– Robert Frost

Silver Lining Moments

By Kerry Raleigh

From raindrops to rainbows
A Silver Lining grows
Sometimes it is hard to see
And we may fall to our knees
Sometimes it shines so bright
That our hearts are filled with light
As clouds drift in and as they move away
Over time we know that every MOMENT
of every day
Has within it a SILVER LINING
that stays

What's your Silver Lining Moment?

A moment of _____ **is lined by** _____.

_____

_____

_____

_____

_____

_____

_____

_____

_____

_____

_____

_____

_____

_____

_____

_____

_____

_____

_____

_____

_____

_____

_____

_____

_____

_____

_____

A moment of _____ **is lined by** _____.

_____

_____

_____

_____

_____

_____

_____

_____

_____

_____

_____

_____

_____

_____

_____

_____

_____

_____

_____

_____

_____

_____

_____

A moment of _____ **is lined by** _____.

A moment of _____ **is lined by** _____.

_____

_____

_____

_____

_____

_____

_____

_____

_____

_____

_____

_____

_____

_____

_____

_____

_____

_____

_____

_____

_____

_____

A moment of _____ **is lined by** _____.

_____

_____

_____

_____

_____

_____

_____

_____

_____

_____

_____

_____

_____

_____

_____

_____

_____

_____

_____

_____

_____

_____

_____

A moment of _____ **is lined by** _____.

_____

_____

_____

_____

_____

_____

_____

_____

_____

_____

_____

_____

_____

_____

_____

_____

_____

_____

_____

_____

_____

_____

_____

_____

_____

_____

A moment of _____ **is lined by** _____.

_____

_____

_____

_____

_____

_____

_____

_____

_____

_____

_____

_____

_____

_____

_____

_____

_____

_____

_____

_____

_____

A moment of _____ is lined by _____.

_____

_____

_____

_____

_____

_____

_____

_____

_____

_____

_____

_____

_____

_____

_____

_____

_____

_____

_____

_____

_____

_____

_____

_____

_____

A moment of _____ is lined by _____.

_____

_____

_____

_____

_____

_____

_____

_____

_____

_____

_____

_____

_____

_____

_____

_____

_____

_____

_____

_____

_____

_____

_____

_____

_____

_____

Gratitude Feeling & Resilience Building

_____

From this moment of _____
lined by _____:

GRATITUDE

I am grateful for: _____

_____

_____

_____

RESILIENCE

My ability to recover from a difficulty, to overcome a challenge, to get
up after a fall – my resilience – is evident in: _____

_____

_____

_____

With gratitude and resilience, _____

_____

_____

_____

"There is a candle in your heart,
ready to be kindled.
There is a void in your soul, ready to be filled.
You feel it, don't you?"
- *Rumi*

A moment of LITTLE MONEY is lined by PROSPERITY

Most people I know who travel to Italy gained weight while they were there. The food is delicious! When I went there for my study abroad, I lost weight. I paid the tuition and study abroad fees through a student loan. I had a very tight budget for actual living— you know, things like eating, drinking, seeing the sights, etc. I absolutely cherish my time there and would not do it differently, but I had very little day to day living money.

In the mornings, I would walk to a little market and get one large bottle of water. I would move to a street stand and get two pieces of bread and one piece of fruit. That would be my breakfast and lunch. Then, I would get a small meal at a restaurant with friends or have a bowl of cereal for dinner. My small meals would usually be an appetizer or side dish. While my friends ordered wine, I drank my water. Every 3-4 days, I would skip the dinner and get a gelato instead.

The restaurants in Italy charged a coperto, a fee to simply sit down at the table. Many times, while my friends and I were out and about, they would stop at a restaurant for lunch. Even though I had my own packed lunch, I could not join them because I could not afford the coperto on a daily basis. So, many times I would simply say that I wanted to walk about and explore the city while they had lunch and we would meet up after their lunch.

Needless to say, my bottle water, 2 pieces of bread, and 1 piece of fruit were important to me. They were my steady source of nourishment.

One afternoon, as I was looking for a bench to sit on and enjoy my lunch of one roll and a peach, an old lady approached me. She held out her hands toward me. I gave her my bread and peach. She sat down and her eyes beamed with delight as she ate the peach. She looked at me and smiled with genuine gratitude – and love. My own hunger went away and was replaced with joy at having been able to share my food with her. I felt rich!

I went to a nearby store to get some water for her. When I came back, she was gone. Now, years later, I don't remember feeling hungry or missing meals, but I do see this old lady's face beaming with love. This fills my spirit and I realize that how rich I am does not depend on how much money is my bank account. One of my poorest times was one of my richest moments. Prosperity comes in many forms.

In the eyes and smile of an old lady, I discovered how a moment of little money is lined by prosperity.

Florence, Italy @ 1997

Gratitude Feeling & Resilience Building

From this moment of little money lined by prosperity:

GRATITUDE

I am grateful for: the smile and shared joy with the elderly lady; having enough to share with others

_____

_____

_____

RESILIENCE

My ability to recover from a difficulty, to overcome a challenge, to get up after a fall – my resilience – is evident in: giving away my lunch and trusting that I would be provided for and I would have enough; focusing on what I could do and have that did not require money instead of focusing on the things that I could not buy with no money.

With gratitude and resilience, I feel free and generous!

_____

_____

_____

"There is nothing ugly; I never saw an ugly thing in my life: for let the form of an object be what it may, -- light, shade, and perspective will always make it beautiful."

- John Constable

Silver Lining Moments

By Kerry Raleigh

From raindrops to rainbows
A Silver Lining grows
Sometimes it is hard to see
And we may fall to our knees
Sometimes it shines so bright
That our hearts are filled with light
As clouds drift in and as they move away
Over time we know that every MOMENT
of every day
Has within it a SILVER LINING
that stays

What's your Silver Lining Moment?

A moment of _____ **is lined by** _____.

_____

_____

_____

_____

_____

_____

_____

_____

_____

_____

_____

_____

_____

_____

_____

_____

_____

_____

_____

_____

_____

_____

_____

_____

A moment of _____ is lined by _____.

_____

_____

_____

_____

_____

_____

_____

_____

_____

_____

_____

_____

_____

_____

_____

_____

_____

_____

_____

_____

_____

_____

_____

A moment of _____ **is lined by** _____.

_____

_____

_____

_____

_____

_____

_____

_____

_____

_____

_____

_____

_____

_____

_____

_____

_____

_____

_____

_____

_____

_____

_____

A moment of _____ **is lined by** _____.

_____

_____

_____

_____

_____

_____

_____

_____

_____

_____

_____

_____

_____

_____

_____

_____

_____

_____

_____

_____

_____

_____

_____

_____

_____

A moment of _____ is lined by _____.

_____

_____

_____

_____

_____

_____

_____

_____

_____

_____

_____

_____

_____

_____

_____

_____

_____

_____

_____

_____

_____

_____

_____

A moment of _____ is lined by _____.

_____

_____

_____

_____

_____

_____

_____

_____

_____

_____

_____

_____

_____

_____

_____

_____

_____

_____

_____

_____

_____

_____

_____

A moment of _____ is lined by _____.

_____

_____

_____

_____

_____

_____

_____

_____

_____

_____

_____

_____

_____

_____

_____

_____

_____

_____

_____

_____

_____

_____

_____

A moment of _____ is lined by _____.

_____
_____
_____
_____
_____
_____
_____
_____
_____
_____
_____
_____
_____
_____
_____
_____
_____
_____
_____
_____
_____
_____
_____
_____
_____

A moment of _____ **is lined by** _____.

_____

_____

_____

_____

_____

_____

_____

_____

_____

_____

_____

_____

_____

_____

_____

_____

_____

_____

_____

_____

_____

_____

_____

_____

Gratitude Feeling & Resilience Building

_____

From this moment of _____
lined by _____:

GRATITUDE

I am grateful for: _____
_____
_____
_____

RESILIENCE

My ability to recover from a difficulty, to overcome a challenge, to get
up after a fall – my resilience – is evident in: _____
_____
_____

With gratitude and resilience, _____
_____
_____

"When angry, count ten before you speak; if very angry a hundred."
- Thomas Jefferson

"When angry, count four; when very angry, swear."
- Mark Twain

A moment of PET PEEVES is lined by CAMARADERIE

This moment took a very conscious and deliberate effort to see the silver lining. And, it is probably one of the most trivial of cloudy moments.

I was at a Costa coffeehouse in Beijing, China. A quick aside, I love coffeehouses. I am the person who goes there to read, write, work, etc. When I went to buy my drink, the barista recognized me and handed me a receipt for a matcha latte before I even ordered. Through the language barrier, he was asking me if I wanted my regular drink. I realized that I had become a regular in my local Beijing coffeehouse – even though the baristas do not speak English and I do not speak Chinese.

This morning, Costa was empty. There was only one other person in the place. After ordering, I sat at a table, away from the other person to give us each some space. I typed away on my laptop. Two men came in and ordered their drinks. Although the place was empty, and there were 20 or more tables to choose from, they chose the table right next to me. They started speaking very loudly to each other. And, one was eating a croissant while he was talking, with bits of croissant flying into the air– with the tables so close, bits of croissant came precariously close to my personal space. This same guy started to drink his coffee. BUT, he did not drink his coffee like every other person on the face of the earth. No, he took his spoon, swirled it filling the air with tings as the spoon nicks the edge of the mug, and then he held the spoon up, and slurped the coffee. Over and over again. And again, and again, and again….

Yackity Yack, Croissant bits flying. Ting, Ting. Slllluuuuurrrrpppp.
Yackity Yack, Croissant bits flying. Ting, Ting. Slllluuuuurrrrpppp.

I was beyond annoyed. Why did they sit at the table that is practically touching my table? I considered glaring at them. I noticeably looked at the other tables with a perplexed expression on my face, which I hoped they would see. Annoyed.

Then, I took a breath. Yes, this is annoying. As I was stewing over this, a quiet inner voice asked "But – what about the barista remembering my drink? That's pretty cool." I was now a regular here. In a city of millions, I was remembered. They acknowledged me here. Pretty cool.

That is the moment that I made the very deliberate decision to focus on the barista recognizing me. As I left Costa that day, I was no longer annoyed or frustrated. Rather, I had a smile on my face, knowing that I had made a connection with my Costa barista. That felt good.

Being tested by my pet peeves did not dampen a sense of connection and camaraderie.

From being recognized by a barista, I discovered how a moment of pet peeves is lined by camaraderie.

Beijing, China @ 2018

Gratitude Feeling & Resilience Building

From this moment of pet peeves is lined by camaraderie:

GRATITUDE

I am grateful for: <u>**matcha tea lattes and being recognized with a smile!**</u>

RESILIENCE

My ability to recover from a difficulty, to overcome a challenge, to get up after a fall – my resilience – is evident in: <u>**resetting being annoyed to being grateful, getting past a pet peeve to appreciate being recognized in a city of millions!**</u>

With gratitude and resilience, <u>**I feel empowered; these tools really do work!**</u>

The sound of coffee and tea lattes

.......*Ohmmmmmmm*
.......*Ahhhhhhhh*
.......*Uhmmmmmm*
.......*Yummmmmmm*

Silver Lining Moments
By Kerry Raleigh

From raindrops to rainbows
A Silver Lining grows
Sometimes it is hard to see
And we may fall to our knees
Sometimes it shines so bright
That our hearts are filled with light
As clouds drift in and as they move away
Over time we know that every MOMENT
of every day
Has within it a SILVER LINING
that stays

What's your Silver Lining Moment?

A moment of _____ **is lined by** _____.

_____

_____

_____

_____

_____

_____

_____

_____

_____

_____

_____

_____

_____

_____

_____

_____

_____

_____

_____

_____

_____

_____

_____

_____

A moment of _____ is lined by _____.

_____

_____

_____

_____

_____

_____

_____

_____

_____

_____

_____

_____

_____

_____

_____

_____

_____

_____

_____

_____

_____

_____

_____

_____

_____

A moment of _____ **is lined by** _____ .

_____

_____

_____

_____

_____

_____

_____

_____

_____

_____

_____

_____

_____

_____

_____

_____

_____

_____

_____

_____

_____

_____

_____

_____

A moment of _____ is lined by _____.

_____

_____

_____

_____

_____

_____

_____

_____

_____

_____

_____

_____

_____

_____

_____

_____

_____

_____

_____

_____

_____

_____

_____

_____

_____

A moment of _____ **is lined by** _____.

_____

_____

_____

_____

_____

_____

_____

_____

_____

_____

_____

_____

_____

_____

_____

_____

_____

_____

_____

_____

_____

_____

A moment of _____ is lined by _____.

_____

_____

_____

_____

_____

_____

_____

_____

_____

_____

_____

_____

_____

_____

_____

_____

_____

_____

_____

_____

_____

_____

_____

_____

_____

A moment of _____ **is lined by** _____.

_____

_____

_____

_____

_____

_____

_____

_____

_____

_____

_____

_____

_____

_____

_____

_____

_____

_____

_____

_____

_____

_____

_____

_____

A moment of _____ is lined by _____.

_____

_____

_____

_____

_____

_____

_____

_____

_____

_____

_____

_____

_____

_____

_____

_____

_____

_____

_____

_____

_____

_____

_____

_____

_____

_____

A moment of _____ **is lined by** _____.

_____

_____

_____

_____

_____

_____

_____

_____

_____

_____

_____

_____

_____

_____

_____

_____

_____

_____

_____

_____

_____

_____

_____

_____

_____

Gratitude Feeling & Resilience Building

_____

From this moment of _____

lined by _____:

GRATITUDE

I am grateful for: _____

_____

_____

_____

RESILIENCE

My ability to recover from a difficulty, to overcome a challenge, to get up after a fall – my resilience – is evident in: _____

_____

_____

_____

With gratitude and resilience, _____

_____

_____

_____

"Make the best use
of what's in your power
and take the rest as it happens."
- *Epictetus*

A moment of OVERLOAD AND LONELINESS is lined by FRIENDSHIP AND TIME

After my first divorce, I wanted to get in shape, volunteer, create a fun social life, and develop a circle of friends. But, at that time, my average work week was well in the high 70 hours, with many weeks having more work hours, and very few weeks having less. I was constantly struggling to meet my firm's billable hour expectations – let alone court deadlines, client needs, and business development. Feeling overwhelmed with wanting to create new and positive things in my life but constricted with time, I kept asking "How will I have time to do all this? Life has got to be more than work, doesn't it?"

Driving home from work, I heard a radio advertisement for Team in Training, a fundraising arm for the Leukemia & Lymphoma Society. Team in Training trains you for a marathon with a team full of coaches and fellow runners, in exchange for your fundraising for the Leukemia & Lymphoma Society. Getting in shape, making new friends, and doing something good for others – I needed to check this out.

I went to their informational meeting, albeit a little late due to work. The training would involve a group run on Saturday mornings and a goal for your individual runs during the week. The fundraising you could do on your time, on your computer – essentially asking friends and family to donate to the Leukemia & Lymphoma Society. I could do this (and thank you to all my friends and family who supported me and donated to the Leukemia & Lymphoma Society)!

I remember the first Saturday run. I tend to feel awkward at new things and around new people. This first Saturday was no different. But all I had to do was run – and they started us with this run and walk pattern. I think we started with a run for 3 minutes, walk for 2. We eventually worked up to run for 8 minutes, walk for 2 minutes. Somehow, as the miles went by on our runs so did my awkwardness. I found myself in a group who would do these Saturday runs together and who convinced me to do the whole marathon as opposed to my initial goal of a half-marathon. Running with this group was fun. We would talk, laugh, complain about running, and then run some more.

Some Saturdays, I would do the Team In Training morning run and then go to the office, which happened to be very close to the downtown West Palm Beach, Florida runs. Because we were in sunny Florida, as the runs got longer, our morning start times got earlier. Towards the end of the training, I think our morning runs started at 4:00 am so that we could finish before the full heat of Florida's sun. And, I am not a morning person.

I was always late when I drove myself and would miss the starting time with the group runs. Luckily, my friend Debbie, who I met through Team in Training, started to pick me up for the Saturday mornings. So, I would go to bed on Friday nights, wearing my running clothes, with my running shoes and socks at the edge of the bed. On the pillow next to me would be a Zone Bar or protein bar. I would set my alarm for an hour and half before Debbie was to pick me up, eat my Zone bar, and then go back to sleep until 15 minutes (okay..10 minutes) before she was to be there. If it wasn't for Debbie, I don't think I would have made the early Saturday runs, and then would not have completed the marathon.

My individual runs during the week went along. Some days, I would just get in the zone and fall back into a breathing pattern I used since college. Right foot forward: "Energize", left foot forward "the body", right foot forward "free", left foot forward "the soul". Over and over again: "Energize the body. Free the soul." Some days, I felt like little birds were flying with me as squirrels joined in the fun. Another day, I almost stepped on little dead animal on the side of the road. Not all runs were peaceful, but each one left me feeling a little bit better.

I had ACL reconstruction surgery when I was 16. Although my knee has been fairly strong all these years after the surgery, the marathon training put it to a test. During our first ½ marathon that we completed as part of the training, my knee gave out on mile 8. I finished the last 5 miles, behind my running buddies. I completed these last five miles one step at a time – with each step saying to myself – I can do one more step: left foot forward "I can do", right foot forward "one more step", over and over again. I finished the ½ marathon but I wasn't sure how I would handle the full marathon in less than a month.

On the day of the marathon, I was prepared to run the marathon by myself. I figured that due to my knee, I would be slower than my teammates. It was okay – I was divorced and alone. I created this whole internal dialogue that I was meant to be alone as I could only count on myself; it was fitting that I do the marathon by myself. This, the marathon would teach me, was bullshit.

I started the marathon with my new-found friends. At different medic stops along the course, I put this gel on my knee and kept going. We ran together; we walked together; we took our bathroom stops together (this was at Disney World and we all used the public restrooms in Disney – none of us too keen on "the peeing as you run tactic" used by some marathoners), we weathered the hot Florida heat even as a few of the water stops ran out of water, and — we crossed the finish line <u>together</u>! Crossing the finish line, I realized that I had to stop telling myself that I couldn't count on others and that I had to be alone. This marathon and my Team in Training friends proved that this was not true!

Another narrative the marathon changed was one that I didn't have time for fun or friends. Even in my 60, 70, 80 hour workweeks, I trained for a marathon, met new friends, created a fun social life, and did something positive. Somehow by adding this to my life, I felt like I had freed up more time, and certainly more joy in my life.

With each mile that I ran, I discovered how a moment of overload and loneliness is lined by friendship and time.

Disney Marathon @ 2007

Gratitude Feeling & Resilience Building

From this moment of overload and loneliness lined by friendship and time:

GRATITUDE

I am grateful for: **Debbie; the little bit of extra time to sleep in, and the entire Team in Training running group; Sunday Fundays; Zone bars; my Mom and my sisters cheering me on at the marathon; new friendships and renewed friendships from years past; the music friends gave me for my training.**

RESILIENCE

My ability to recover from a difficulty, to overcome a challenge, to get up after a fall – my resilience – is evident in: **not quitting when my knee gave out; getting up at 3:30 am to go running – to go running!!!**

With gratitude and resilience, **I feel connected to and supported by others**

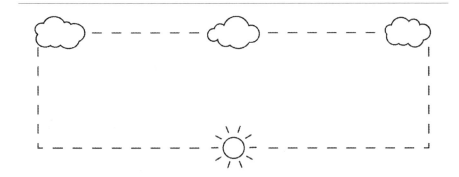

Silver Lining Moments

By Kerry Raleigh

From raindrops to rainbows
A Silver Lining grows
Sometimes it is hard to see
And we may fall to our knees
Sometimes it shines so bright
That our hearts are filled with light
As clouds drift in and as they move away
Over time we know that every MOMENT
of every day
Has within it a SILVER LINING
that stays

What's your Silver Lining Moment?

A moment of _____ **is lined by** _____.

_____

_____

_____

_____

_____

_____

_____

_____

_____

_____

_____

_____

_____

_____

_____

_____

_____

_____

_____

_____

_____

_____

_____

_____

_____

A moment of _____ is lined by _____.

A moment of _____ is lined by _____.

_____

_____

_____

_____

_____

_____

_____

_____

_____

_____

_____

_____

_____

_____

_____

_____

_____

_____

_____

_____

_____

_____

_____

_____

A moment of _____ is lined by _____.

A moment of _____ is lined by _____.

_____

_____

_____

_____

_____

_____

_____

_____

_____

_____

_____

_____

_____

_____

_____

_____

_____

_____

_____

_____

_____

A moment of _____ is lined by _____.

_____

_____

_____

_____

_____

_____

_____

_____

_____

_____

_____

_____

_____

_____

_____

_____

_____

_____

_____

_____

_____

_____

_____

_____

A moment of _____ is lined by _____.

_____

_____

_____

_____

_____

_____

_____

_____

_____

_____

_____

_____

_____

_____

_____

_____

_____

_____

_____

_____

_____

_____

_____

A moment of _____ is lined by _____.

_____

_____

_____

_____

_____

_____

_____

_____

_____

_____

_____

_____

_____

_____

_____

_____

_____

_____

_____

_____

_____

_____

_____

_____

A moment of _____ **is lined by** _____.

_____

_____

_____

_____

_____

_____

_____

_____

_____

_____

_____

_____

_____

_____

_____

_____

_____

_____

_____

_____

_____

_____

_____

_____

Gratitude Feeling & Resilience Building

_____

From this moment of _____
lined by _____:

GRATITUDE

I am grateful for: _____

_____

_____

_____

RESILIENCE

My ability to recover from a difficulty, to overcome a challenge, to get
up after a fall – my resilience – is evident in: _____

_____

_____

_____

With gratitude and resilience, _____

_____

_____

_____

"And even in our sleep,
pain which cannot forget falls drop by drop
upon the heart until, in our own despair,
against our will, comes wisdom
through the awful grace of God."
- *Aeschylus*

A moment of EXHAUSTION is lined by a STRANGER'S SUPPORT and HUMOR

My lawyer days were often long, stressful, and demanding. When I got a break, I slept. This was also before WiFi on planes. So, with no internet, no emails, no phone calls, I usually fell asleep before takeoff.

On this one particular flight, I was sitting in the aisle seat. True to form, I quickly fell asleep. I turned toward the aisle with my head resting over my left shoulder. A bit later, I woke up facing the window with my head on the shoulder of the guy sitting in the middle seat. I was embarrassed and apologized. He said not to worry about it.

I turned back to the aisle. I fell back asleep with my head once again resting over my left shoulder. A bit later, I woke up again....with my head on the shoulder of the guy next to me. I again apologized. He again said it was okay.

I turned back to the aisle again. I fell back asleep with my head facing the aisle and resting over my left shoulder again. And, a bit later, I woke up for a third time...with my head <u>and</u> my hand on this guy's shoulder as if his shoulder was my pillow. As I was starting to apologize and turn to the aisle again, he told me not to worry about it and to just sleep.

As the plane was starting its descent, I woke up feeling well rested and refreshed. The guy next to me simply smiled and joked, in a completely non-creepy but funny way, "I usually have to take a girl out to dinner before she will sleep with me".

On a plane, I discovered how a moment of exhaustion is lined by a stranger's support and humor.

Somewhere in the sky @ 2010

135

Gratitude Feeling & Resilience Building

From this moment of exhaustion lined by a stranger's support and humor:

GRATITUDE

I am grateful for: **the kindness of strangers, quick wit and good humor; good sleep.**

RESILIENCE

My ability to recover from a difficulty, to overcome a challenge, to get up after a fall – my resilience – is evident in: **laughing at myself and the situation**

With gratitude and resilience, **I feel happy and recharged.**

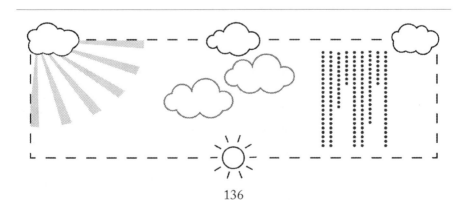

Silver Lining Moments

By Kerry Raleigh

From raindrops to rainbows
A Silver Lining grows
Sometimes it is hard to see
And we may fall to our knees
Sometimes it shines so bright
That our hearts are filled with light
As clouds drift in and as they move away
Over time we know that every MOMENT
of every day
Has within it a SILVER LINING
that stays

What's your Silver Lining Moment?

A moment of _____ is lined by _____.

_____

_____

_____

_____

_____

_____

_____

_____

_____

_____

_____

_____

_____

_____

_____

_____

_____

_____

_____

_____

_____

_____

_____

_____

_____

A moment of _____ is lined by _____.

_____

_____

_____

_____

_____

_____

_____

_____

_____

_____

_____

_____

_____

_____

_____

_____

_____

_____

_____

_____

_____

_____

_____

_____

A moment of _____ **is lined by** _____.

_____

_____

_____

_____

_____

_____

_____

_____

_____

_____

_____

_____

_____

_____

_____

_____

_____

_____

_____

_____

_____

_____

_____

A moment of _____ **is lined by** _____.

_____

_____

_____

_____

_____

_____

_____

_____

_____

_____

_____

_____

_____

_____

_____

_____

_____

_____

_____

_____

_____

_____

_____

_____

_____

A moment of _____ **is lined by** _____.

_____

_____

_____

_____

_____

_____

_____

_____

_____

_____

_____

_____

_____

_____

_____

_____

_____

_____

_____

_____

_____

_____

A moment of _____ is lined by _____.

_____

_____

_____

_____

_____

_____

_____

_____

_____

_____

_____

_____

_____

_____

_____

_____

_____

_____

_____

_____

_____

_____

_____

_____

_____

A moment of _____ is lined by _____.

A moment of _____ is lined by _____.

_____

_____

_____

_____

_____

_____

_____

_____

_____

_____

_____

_____

_____

_____

_____

_____

_____

_____

_____

_____

_____

_____

_____

_____

A moment of _____ **is lined by** _____.

_____

_____

_____

_____

_____

_____

_____

_____

_____

_____

_____

_____

_____

_____

_____

_____

_____

_____

_____

_____

_____

_____

_____

_____

_____

Gratitude Feeling & Resilience Building

_____

From this moment of _____

lined by _____:

GRATITUDE

I am grateful for: _____

_____

_____

_____

RESILIENCE

My ability to recover from a difficulty, to overcome a challenge, to get up after a fall – my resilience – is evident in: _____

_____

_____

With gratitude and resilience, _____

_____

_____

_____

"Laugh
because that is the purest sound."
- Hafez (aka Hafiz)

A moment of a FRENZIED HURRY is lined by a CHILD'S POSITIVE INSIGHT

It is rare for my two sisters (Kathy and Kelly) and I to be in the same city at the same time, which is a shame because we truly have so much fun with each other and are very close. My sisters are my best friends. This is a little side note that has nothing to do with this story other than this moment involves my sisters.

So, here we are on a cold winter day in Ohio. Kath and I are at Kelly's house having spent the night there. The 3 of us and Kelly's 3 daughters had the whole morning and early afternoon free. With no plans until about 3 or 4 in the afternoon, we kept saying how we could relax and that we had so much time on our hands. There was plenty of time to get ready up until the point when there was no more time to get ready. Sure enough, in the final 15 minutes before we were supposed to leave, we were all rushing, getting ready, and gathering up our stuff; we created a frenzy storm that can only happen when 6 people each give themselves 15 minutes to do what normally takes 30 minutes.

Finally, we were all piled in the car, my sisters, my nieces, and I--albeit 15 minutes later than when we had wanted to leave. As we were pulling out the driveway, my sister checked with my niece as to whether she had taken her medicine. She hadn't. Lamenting over whether it would be okay for her to be late on her afternoon dose (it was an antibiotic for some cough), she kept driving. When we got a few miles away, my sister was continuing with her checklist with the girls. They had forgot to bring something that we needed with us.

As she was turning around to go back to the house, we were focusing on how this was going to make us even later. Frustration and stress were beginning to fill the car. Right away, my niece piped up that at least her sister could take her medicine on time. And, that reset the energy in the car. All the angst, frustration, and stress of rushing around just flew out the window. And, I beamed with pride for my niece and her ability to instantly see the silver lining of the moment.

Yes, we were going to be later than we had hoped. However, we created this "late" energy along with the rushing, stress, and should-haves that so often accompany being late. In our reset, we could see that being 15 minutes later than we anticipated would not affect our dinner plans with our parents. It was okay if dinner was a little later than we had planned.

We went back to the house. My one niece got her medicine. My other nieces got the stuff they needed. As we drove off the second time, the car was filled with laughter and light-hearted conversation. The frenzied hurried stress was reset by my niece's positive insight.

In a mini-van with family, I discovered how a moment of a frenzied hurry is lined by a child's positive insight.

Aurora, Ohio @ January 2018

Gratitude Feeling & Resilience Building

_____

From this moment of a frenzied hurry lined by a child's positive insight:

GRATITUDE

I am grateful for: **family; my sisters, my parents, my nieces and nephews;**

_____

_____

_____

RESILIENCE

My ability to recover from a difficulty, to overcome a challenge, to get up after a fall – my resilience – is evident in: **letting go stressful energy and resetting with laughter.**

_____

_____

With gratitude and resilience, **I am at ease and having fun; I enjoy being with my family**

_____

_____

Silver Lining Moments

By Kerry Raleigh

From raindrops to rainbows
A Silver Lining grows
Sometimes it is hard to see
And we may fall to our knees
Sometimes it shines so bright
That our hearts are filled with light
As clouds drift in and as they move away
Over time we know that every MOMENT
of every day
Has within it a SILVER LINING
that stays

What's your Silver Lining Moment?

A moment of _____ **is lined by** _____.

_____

_____

_____

_____

_____

_____

_____

_____

_____

_____

_____

_____

_____

_____

_____

_____

_____

_____

_____

_____

_____

_____

_____

_____

A moment of _____ **is lined by** _____.

_____

_____

_____

_____

_____

_____

_____

_____

_____

_____

_____

_____

_____

_____

_____

_____

_____

_____

_____

_____

_____

_____

_____

A moment of _____ **is lined by** _____.

_____

_____

_____

_____

_____

_____

_____

_____

_____

_____

_____

_____

_____

_____

_____

_____

_____

_____

_____

_____

_____

_____

_____

A moment of _____ is lined by _____.

_____

_____

_____

_____

_____

_____

_____

_____

_____

_____

_____

_____

_____

_____

_____

_____

_____

_____

_____

_____

_____

_____

_____

_____

_____

A moment of _____ is lined by _____.

_____

_____

_____

_____

_____

_____

_____

_____

_____

_____

_____

_____

_____

_____

_____

_____

_____

_____

_____

_____

_____

_____

_____

_____

_____

_____

A moment of _____ **is lined by** _____.

_____

_____

_____

_____

_____

_____

_____

_____

_____

_____

_____

_____

_____

_____

_____

_____

_____

_____

_____

_____

_____

_____

_____

_____

_____

A moment of _____ **is lined by** _____.

_____

_____

_____

_____

_____

_____

_____

_____

_____

_____

_____

_____

_____

_____

_____

_____

_____

_____

_____

_____

_____

_____

A moment of _____ **is lined by** _____.

_____

_____

_____

_____

_____

_____

_____

_____

_____

_____

_____

_____

_____

_____

_____

_____

_____

_____

_____

_____

_____

_____

_____

_____

A moment of _____ is lined by _____.

_____

_____

_____

_____

_____

_____

_____

_____

_____

_____

_____

_____

_____

_____

_____

_____

_____

_____

_____

_____

_____

_____

_____

Gratitude Feeling & Resilience Building

_____

From this moment of _____
lined by _____:

GRATITUDE

I am grateful for: _____
_____
_____
_____

RESILIENCE

My ability to recover from a difficulty, to overcome a challenge, to get
up after a fall – my resilience – is evident in: _____
_____
_____
_____

With gratitude and resilience, _____
_____
_____
_____

"Crying does not indicate that you are weak. Since birth, it has always been a sign that you are alive."
- *Charlotte Brontë*

A moment of DEATH is lined by LIFE

It was around midnight on a Sunday night in May 2018, when my friend Lori messaged me to call her right away. This was unusual. Lori's message added "it's about Mamie". I walked into another room so I could call Lori in private, fearing that my friend Mamie was seriously injured or sick. Lori, blessedly blunt because there is no good way to say what she had to say, simply said "Mamie's dead".

I saw Mamie's Facebook Live from earlier that day showing her and her husband Greg hiking in the Panamanian mountains. She was smiling, full of life, as Mamie always is. She is dead. Lori explained that as Mamie and Greg were ending their hike (not long after Mamie's Facebook video post), it began to storm and there was lightning. At the very second when Mamie opened her car door, lightning struck the car or lightning struck an electrical wire that struck the car. I am not sure of the exact details, but Mamie was electrocuted by lightning and died. I was too shocked to say anything close to appropriate to Lori. I focused on the details as my mind was working to grasp the full weight of the permanence of this sentence – Mamie is dead.

And, from that sentence, my mind and emotions began this loop of thoughts. Mamie, my friend who fully embraced life, died. Mamie, who would laugh loudly, tell you like it is, and go on adventures, died. Mamie, who came to watch an Ohio State v. Michigan game with me while I was going through my divorce, even when she was juggling work, being a foster mom, and had a lot going on in her life, died. Mamie, who believed in the kindness and love in me, died. Mamie who was one-half of the Mamie and Greg duo who showed me how a relationship grounded in love, built on respect, and filled with fun could look, died. Mamie died. What???

I thought about my last visit with Mamie about 8 months earlier. I visited Mamie and Greg in Panama at their hostel. They had cheered me on through my Pause and Reset Journey and now my Journey took me to them. I took Mamie's fitness classes and could see how much her students loved her as she kicked our butts! I took her yoga class and was grounded as I did the tree pose and looked out a window overlooking trees. She took a group of us out on the river where we soaked in natural hot springs. Mamie and I sat on their back porch, drinking wine, talking about everything and nothing, laughing and crying a bit. Gregarious, loud, and fun Mamie turned toward me for a second, looked me in the eye, and softly implored me to see my own goodness and worthiness of love. Then, she added, in a loud shrill mixing laughter and loudness, "I mean it, Kerry. I mean it!!" But, now, Mamie's dead.

Mamie was just 40, maybe 41, possibly 39, when she died. She rescued a greyhound dog and adopted a cat. She worked full-time but still managed to find time to volunteer and help those with HIV. She went to Oktoberfest in Germany, to St. Patrick's Day in Ireland, and to the world's largest tomato fight in Spain. She organized these trips with friends, making and sharing adventures with those in her life. She got her chest painted at Fantasy Fest in Key West. She organized parties and outings. During the Olympics, she created her own version of Olympic-games for some fun competition among friends. She completed mud runs. She was an avid Ohio State Buckeyes fan. She was a mentor to teenage girls. (At a celebration of Mamie's life, one of the girls shared how Mamie helped her buy an outfit and jewelry for her first formal dance and how, whenever she felt alone, Mamie was always there for her.) Mamie married a man who truly was her partner in life. They became foster parents to multiple children over a period of a few years. They moved to Panama and opened a hostel where guests from all over the world commented how Mamie and Greg's hostel was a home away from home, filled with community and friendship.

And, she did it all loudly, boldly, and with an overflowing sense of fun that literally spread smiles across the world.

As I write this, I feel compelled to share a message from Mamie. When Mamie and Greg were foster parents, they were part of the program that helped parents learn parenting skills and have their kids returned to them. Mamie and Greg knew they would love these children who would ultimately be taken away from them. One time, Mamie shared with me how it frustrated her when people told her they could never do what she and Greg were doing because they were not strong enough. Mamie looked at me, and said, and I am paraphrasing because this conversation was a few years ago, "I am not stronger than them. It hurts –a lot – when we return the kids to the parents. It feels like we are losing our kids. I am not strong when I do this; I am sad. It's hard, Kerry! It's hard!! But it is not about us; it's about the kids and the parents and helping families be healthy families. And, we get to provide the love that is the foundation for this!" If anyone reading this has considered becoming foster parents but haven't because they thought it would be too hard to let go of the kids, think of Mamie. Yes, it will be hard but love will get you through the hardship. And, this is straight from Mamie.

The cloud over Mamie's death hung over me for quite some time with that thought-loop going around and around in my head and my heart. I started writing this four months ago but I could not finish it because I couldn't see the silver lining. However, I knew it would come; I just needed to be patient with myself as I grieved for my friend. Two nights ago, right before I fell asleep, it came to me: Mamie's death is lined with life. She lived fully. She laughed fully. She loved fully.

Now, as I write about her death, Mamie continues to inspire and empower me to live fully, laugh fully, and love fully. She lives on in each of us who were lucky enough to know her.

**From my friend Mamie, I discovered how
a moment of death is lined by life.**

Jupiter, Florida, Aurora, Ohio, & Weaverville, NC @ 2018

Gratitude Feeling & Resilience Building

From this moment of death lined by life:

GRATITUDE

I am grateful for: **having the privilege of being Mamie's friend and the friends I met through her; my friend Lori who shared all life's big moments – both good and bad – since college; for camaraderie and friendships strengthened and formed while watching Ohio State Buckeyes and other college football games at Bru's Room; all my friends; LOVE, LAUGHTER, & LIFE!**

RESILIENCE

My ability to recover from a difficulty, to overcome a challenge, to get up after a fall – my resilience – is evident in: **celebrating Mamie's life and friendship; taking a chance with my Pause & Reset Journey (which was emboldened knowing that –at the same time, Mamie and Greg were doing their own reset in Panama and Lori was doing her reset into acting and writing in California. (There is something in that Mamie, Lori, and I all made big life changes at the same time; something that lives beyond death.)**

With gratitude and resilience, **I feel love and loved; I feel inspired and brave.**

Silver Lining Moments

By Kerry Raleigh

From raindrops to rainbows
A Silver Lining grows
Sometimes it is hard to see
And we may fall to our knees
Sometimes it shines so bright
That our hearts are filled with light
As clouds drift in and as they move away
Over time we know that every MOMENT
of every day
Has within it a SILVER LINING
that stays

What's your Silver Lining Moment?

A moment of _____ **is lined by** _____.

_____

_____

_____

_____

_____

_____

_____

_____

_____

_____

_____

_____

_____

_____

_____

_____

_____

_____

_____

_____

A moment of _____ is lined by _____.

A moment of _____ is lined by _____.

_____

_____

_____

_____

_____

_____

_____

_____

_____

_____

_____

_____

_____

_____

_____

_____

_____

_____

_____

_____

_____

_____

_____

A moment of _____ **is lined by** _____.

_____

_____

_____

_____

_____

_____

_____

_____

_____

_____

_____

_____

_____

_____

_____

_____

_____

_____

_____

_____

_____

_____

_____

A moment of _____ **is lined by** _____.

A moment of _____ **is lined by** _____.

_____

_____

_____

_____

_____

_____

_____

_____

_____

_____

_____

_____

_____

_____

_____

_____

_____

_____

_____

_____

_____

_____

_____

_____

A moment of _____ is lined by _____.

_____

_____

_____

_____

_____

_____

_____

_____

_____

_____

_____

_____

_____

_____

_____

_____

_____

_____

_____

_____

_____

_____

_____

_____

A moment of _____ is lined by _____.

_____

_____

_____

_____

_____

_____

_____

_____

_____

_____

_____

_____

_____

_____

_____

_____

_____

_____

_____

_____

_____

_____

_____

_____

A moment of _____ **is lined by** _____.

_____

_____

_____

_____

_____

_____

_____

_____

_____

_____

_____

_____

_____

_____

_____

_____

_____

_____

_____

_____

_____

_____

Gratitude Feeling & Resilience Building

_____

From this moment of _____
lined by _____:

GRATITUDE

I am grateful for: _____

_____

_____

_____

RESILIENCE

My ability to recover from a difficulty, to overcome a challenge, to get
up after a fall – my resilience – is evident in: _____

_____

_____

_____

With gratitude and resilience, _____

_____

_____

_____

"The gem cannot be
polished without friction,
nor man perfected without trials."
- *Confucius*

A moment of DOUBT is lined by TRUST

_____

Since you picked up this *Silver Lining Moments* journal, you are most likely familiar with some or all of the following: Brené Brown, Dr. Wayne Dyer, *The Secret*, Abram Hicks, Mike Dooley, The Universe Talks, Louise Hays, *The Science of Getting Rich* by Wallace Wattles, Dr. Joyce Myers, biblical scriptures, kinesiology, psychology and how they all state, in their own way, the power of thoughts and our power to heal and choose our thoughts and our lives. For me, so many sources leading to the same conclusion tells me that the conclusion is true. *Silver Lining Moments* Journal is an extension of these. It is another way to practice gratitude and resilience.

I have worked hard and have continued practicing choosing healthy thoughts and affirmations and healing the emotional wounds that formed my self-defeating thoughts. I had core beliefs of not being good enough for love, for success, for happiness, for prosperity, etc., of having to work harder than others to prove myself, and to be perfect to show my value. At some point, my life got so out of whack with my inner self that I no longer trusted myself to know what I needed for my highest and best self. Over the years, I have worked with therapists, wrote in journals, meditated, prayed, exercised, worked through various books and activities, and attended personal development retreats. With my Pause & Reset Journey, I have furthered this healing as I jumped into loving life and trusting the support of God and the Universe. I have reclaimed myself! But….yes, there is a but.

In the summer of 2018, I was two and half years into my Pause and Reset Journey and I found myself living with, and depending on, family while still transitioning to living my purposeful life. I am extremely grateful and feel very blessed to have my family's support. However, this also exposed some lingering, self-defeating, core thoughts - ones that I thought I had healed and replaced with self-love and light.

While staying with my parents, my Dad and I got into a fight over politics. Afterwards, I berated myself for this fight. Instead of a compassionate and wise adult, I turned back into a defensive and argumentative child. With this, a little inner voice called my growth into question by saying "After this whole journey and all your healing and you still get defensive and argumentative. Huh! You haven't learned anything; you haven't grown any!"

A few months later, I thought I had caught up on my finances and was ready to prosper. Then, an unexpected medical bill set me back. And, then an unexpected tax bill seemed to mock me as if to say "Other people can be prosperous but not you. You, you will not break free from financial stress." This thought was a bit sneaky because it seemed to be based on some evidence – actual financial bills – but really it was just another form of not feeling worthy or good enough for prosperity.

I spent my time and thoughts scrambling around looking for ways to earn additional income so I could get ahead of the financial curveballs once and for all. The more I scrambled to find ways for extra money, the less time, energy, and focus I had to work on this journal. I was neglecting my passion as I was letting my frustration with finances fill my thoughts and frustrate my life. And, with these, self-doubt flooded in like a tidal wave. Maybe I don't have what it takes to follow through with my ideas? Maybe I am just talk but not substance? Why do I think that my words in my journal or in my podcast can help others when I am still stuck myself? Ah yes…you little sneak…here you are again… maybe I am not good enough?

But, even here, in this summer and fall of 2018 where these self-doubting, self-defeating, negative beliefs surfaced, are silver lining moments:

- I recognized these thoughts and feelings as they were coming up. Because I recognized them, I didn't get stuck in them and I drew upon the tools that I learned from all the work I have done in the past to reset these thoughts. My previous work and my Pause & Reset Journey were not wasted; they continue to serve me now.

- I got to practice compassion with myself. My instinct is to be hard on myself for not having compassion, wisdom, positive energy, and positive thoughts all the time – for not always feeling these as a natural part of my core self. This compassion is a form of self-love.

- My healing work up to this point focused on my miscarriages, divorces, and being molested as a child because they were such devastating sources of pain. I had to focus on them. I am now seeing other areas that need attention and healing. This is good for a few reasons. One, it shows how far I have come. Two, now I can work on issues that may be even closer to the core. As I heal these, watch the light shine stronger and farther inward and outward!

- These self-defeating thoughts popped up but they were not overpowering and did not linger for very long. They could not block my ultimate trust that I am supported, that I am meant to prosper, and that I can and will use creativity to make a positive impact in the world. <u>And, this trust was not darkened by the cloud of self-doubt because I still saw signs of support.</u>

Here are just a few of those signs of support:

I teach English online. During one of my English classes, my student talked about his Geometry homework. I commented how I would like to re-learn Geometry as I could not do the simple problems he shared with me. I got off the computer and mentioned this to my friend, Debbie, who I was visiting at the time. She told me to wait one second, went into the other room, and returned with a Geometry book for me. Wow – am I powerful! I wished for a Geometry book and I got one in less than an hour!

At the same friend's house, when I walked into the guest bedroom, I commented on a framed quote she has on her wall. It was this quote from F. Scott Fitzgerald:

> She was beautiful, but not like those girls in the magazines. She was beautiful, for the way she thought. She was beautiful, for the sparkle in her eyes when she talked about something she loved. She was beautiful, for her ability to make other people smile, even if she was sad. No, she wasn't beautiful for something as temporary as her looks. She was beautiful, deep down to her soul. She is beautiful.

I commented on what a wonderful way to describe a woman's beauty and how I would like to be described like that by someone. An hour later, as I was lying in bed, I received a message from another friend, Beth, who I had not heard from for a long time. In her message, she sent me this quote and said that it reminded her of me. *Wow – how cool is that?*

My then boyfriend, now fiancé*, and soon to be husband, was in England with his family for the first part of the summer while I was with my family in Ohio. There were many times when he would call just as I was thinking of him. And, now go back to that first sentence in this paragraph – my fiancé and soon to be husband. What greater evidence of my healing than my being in a healthy and happy relationship that is grounded in unconditional love and respect and that is filled with laughter. As I think about us, I am reminded of what I wrote in my journals years ago when I was struggling in unhealthy marriages. I wrote positive affirmations as to the type of relationship I wanted. Those marriages had to end because they could not become this type of relationship. The healing and self-growth from the divorces put me in a place where I would attract and be attracted to the person with whom I could have this relationship. I look at my relationship with my fiancé, the positive affirmations – that I wrote in my journals years before we met – describe us.

I wrote this Silver Lining Moment story while house and pet sitting in Weaverville, North Carolina with my then fiancé. One afternoon, as we were sitting on a porch swing that overlooks the rolling hills of the Blue Ridge Mountains, my fiancé looked at me and said: "Look how lucky we are – we found each other in China and now we get to stay at such a beautiful place." I looked at him, then at the mountains, and soaked it all in – **gratitude**.

The summer and fall of 2018 show me that when self-doubt and self-defeating thoughts creep back in, they no longer derail me. My reset is quicker and fuller – **resilience**.

I can trust in love – in all forms. I can trust in myself and from my past healing. I can trust that I am supported by God and the Universe.

Through the ups and downs of life, I discovered how a moment of doubt is lined by trust.

Jupiter, Florida, Aurora, Ohio, & Weaverville, NC @ 2018

*Shortly after I wrote this story, Rob and I decided to get married right there on that beautiful porch. With the help of two close friends, Caroline and Jessica, and with some serendipity, everything fell into place. Family and friends from across the USA, the UK, Australia, and China all joined in via Zoom and Facebook Live. (This is before Covid…so I am not sure, but we may have had one of the first online marriage ceremonies. ☺)

"Just trust yourself
and you'll learn the art of living."
- *Johann Wolfgang von Goethe*

Gratitude Feeling & Resilience Building

From this moment of doubt lined by trust:

GRATITUDE

I am grateful for: serendipity - good coincidences and timing; Beth and her message with F. Scott Fitzgerald quote; Debbie's Geometry book; my Dad and how our arguments show me how and where I can grow and learn; all the hiccups of this summer and fall of 2018 => and the opportunity to put my tools and beliefs to the test!

RESILIENCE

My ability to recover from a difficulty, to overcome a challenge, to get up after a fall – my resilience – is evident in: not getting stuck in the mud of negativity; talking with my Dad after our argument in peace and with love and understanding my triggers; being excited with the Geometry book; the F. Scott Fitzgerald quote; keeping on -keeping on :)

With gratitude and resilience, I feel true. I step into possibility and dreams. I dance.

"Do not judge yourself harshly. Without mercy for ourselves, we cannot love the world."

— Guatama Buddha

Silver Lining Moments

By Kerry Raleigh

From raindrops to rainbows
A Silver Lining grows
Sometimes it is hard to see
And we may fall to our knees
Sometimes it shines so bright
That our hearts are filled with light
As clouds drift in and as they move away
Over time we know that every MOMENT
of every day
Has within it a SILVER LINING
that stays

What's your Silver Lining Moment?

A moment of _____ is lined by _____.

_____

_____

_____

_____

_____

_____

_____

_____

_____

_____

_____

_____

_____

_____

_____

_____

_____

_____

_____

_____

_____

_____

_____

_____

A moment of _____ **is lined by** _____.

A moment of _____ **is lined by** _____.

_____

_____

_____

_____

_____

_____

_____

_____

_____

_____

_____

_____

_____

_____

_____

_____

_____

_____

_____

_____

_____

_____

_____

_____

A moment of _____ **is lined by** _____.

_____

_____

_____

_____

_____

_____

_____

_____

_____

_____

_____

_____

_____

_____

_____

_____

_____

_____

_____

_____

_____

_____

_____

_____

_____

_____

_____

_____

A moment of _____ **is lined by** _____.

_____

_____

_____

_____

_____

_____

_____

_____

_____

_____

_____

_____

_____

_____

_____

_____

_____

_____

_____

_____

_____

_____

_____

A moment of _____ is lined by _____.

_____

_____

_____

_____

_____

_____

_____

_____

_____

_____

_____

_____

_____

_____

_____

_____

_____

_____

_____

_____

_____

_____

A moment of _____ **is lined by** _____.

_____

_____

_____

_____

_____

_____

_____

_____

_____

_____

_____

_____

_____

_____

_____

_____

_____

_____

_____

_____

_____

_____

A moment of _____ is lined by _____.

_____

_____

_____

_____

_____

_____

_____

_____

_____

_____

_____

_____

_____

_____

_____

_____

_____

_____

_____

_____

_____

_____

_____

_____

_____

A moment of _____ **is lined by** _____.

_____

_____

_____

_____

_____

_____

_____

_____

_____

_____

_____

_____

_____

_____

_____

_____

_____

_____

_____

_____

_____

_____

_____

_____

Gratitude Feeling & Resilience Building

_____

From this moment of _____
lined by _____ :

GRATITUDE

I am grateful for: _____

_____

_____

_____

RESILIENCE

My ability to recover from a difficulty, to overcome a challenge, to get
up after a fall – my resilience – is evident in: _____

_____

_____

_____

With gratitude and resilience, _____

_____

_____

_____

"I wish I could show you when you are lonely or in darkness the astonishing light of your own being."
- Hafez (aka Hafiz)

You are light.

You are love.

Celebrate the silver linings of all your moments!

Congratulations on completing your *Silver Lining Moments* Journal! I am very grateful for you. May you be blessed. May you prosper. May you be filled with compassion and wisdom. May you see and celebrate all your Silver Lining Moments.

About the Author

_____

Kerry Raleigh is the creator of:
- The podcast: Silver Lining Moments with Kerry
- *Silver Lining Moments: A Practice of Gratitude and Resilience*
- The BEING Journals available on Amazon

After experiencing two losses in a series of losses that were the proverbial straw that broke the camel's back, in February 2016, Kerry headed out on what she calls her PAUSE & RESET Journey with two simple goals: (1) reset her life, and (2) expand love and light while having fun. She volunteered with disabled children with Mother Teresa's Missionaries of Charity, as an English tutor with INEB's School of English for Engaged Social Service, as a retail clerk at an Oxfam charity store, and as a field worker on organic farms. She traveled to India, Thailand, Singapore, Sri Lanka, Tibet, England, Scotland, France, Germany, and China, where she met her husband, Rob. Throughout 2018 and 2019, Rob and Kerry traveled by house/pet-sitting in the USA, Canada, Bulgaria, Australia, Greece, and England. If you have a minute (or several), Kerry will share how this Journey is evidence of the love in the Universe and the good in people everywhere.

While in Thailand, Kerry got clarity with her life's purpose and passion. She wants to use creativity for good, to expand love and light with fun and laughter, and to restore and popularize humanity's sense of stewardship for ourselves, for each other, for all animals, for the environment and our planet. No small vision. She knows "the what" she wants to do and trusts that "how" will come. Silver Lining Moments and The BEING Journals are part of this purpose.

Other titles that Kerry has held include weeder, amusement park worker, telemarketer, hospital janitor, and retail salesperson; other hats she wears include lawyer, ESL teacher, podcaster, and writer; and other roles she holds most dear are wife, daughter, sister, aunt, and friend.

CONTACT & CONNECTION LINKS:

LinkedIn: Kerry Raleigh
https://www.linkedin.com/in/kerryraleigh/

Podcast: Silver Lining Moments with Kerry
https://silverliningmoments.libsyn.com/

Instagram: kerryraleigh/SLM & The BEING Journals
https://www.instagram.com/kerryraleigh/

Facebook: The Being Journals
https://www.facebook.com/The-Being-Journals-110004154255634/?view_public_for=110004154255634

Website: www.SilverLiningMoments.com
Email: Kerry@SilverLiningMoments.com

Printed in the United States
by Baker & Taylor Publisher Services